WHAT'S COOKING?

page 2

page 16

Jan Burchett
and Sara Vogler

Story illustrated by
Javier Joaquin

Heinemann

Find out about

- All the strange things people do with food

Tricky words

- buildings
- chocolate
- sculptures
- Yorkshire puddings
- tomato
- Sumo wrestlers
- ostrich

Introduce these tricky words and help the reader when they come across them later!

Text starter

People do very strange things with food. They build with it, they make pictures with it, they even fight with it! Sometimes they eat it – lots and lots of it!

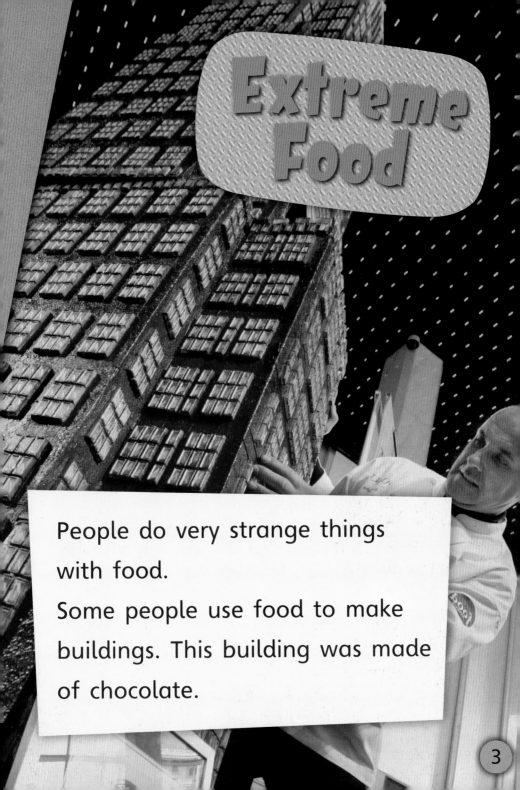

Extreme Food

People do very strange things with food.
Some people use food to make buildings. This building was made of chocolate.

Some people use food to
make pictures.
This picture of a man is made
of food.

Some people use food to make sculptures.
This sculpture is made of pumpkin!
The chef cut the pumpkin to make the sculpture.

Some people like to throw food! Every year, people throw black puddings at a pile of Yorkshire puddings.

Yorkshire Pudding is like a plain pancake.

OFFICIAL WORLD BLACK PUDDING THROWING

The winner is the person who knocks down the most Yorkshire puddings.

Some people like to fight with food. Every year in Spain there is a tomato fight. About 2,000 people throw tomatoes at each other. There is no winner, just lots of messy people!

Some people like to eat lots and lots of food. Sumo wrestlers eat lots of food.

They have to be fat to fight.

A Sumo wrestler eats this for lunch!

And after that – he has pudding!
Then a Sumo wrestler sleeps for
three hours. He has to sleep so that
all the food can turn to fat.

Some animals like to eat strange things. An ostrich in a zoo ate some very strange things!

The zoo took an X-ray of the ostrich and they saw that it had eaten a clock!

I wonder if the clock kept ticking inside the ostrich?

There is a strange man who eats anything. He has eaten two beds and a computer!

He has eaten 7 TVs and 18 bikes.
The biggest thing that he has eaten
is an aeroplane!

People do very strange things with food. One man sat in a bath of baked beans for over 100 hours! How strange is that?

Quiz

Text Detective

- What strange things do people do with food?
- Which food do you think is the strangest?

Word Detective

- **Phonic Focus:** Long vowel phonemes

  Page 3: Sound out the three phonemes in 'food'.

  What long vowel phoneme can you hear?
- Page 7: Can you find three small words in 'tomatoes'?
- Page 10: Find a word that means 'unusual'.

Super Speller

Read these words:

throw fight sleep

Now try to spell them!

HA! HA! HA!

Q What's the best day to eat bacon and eggs?

A Fry-day!

In this story

 Harry

 The chef

The Queen

Introduce these tricky words and help the reader when they come across them later!

Tricky words

- chef
- quiet
- vegetables
- boring

- palace
- frying pan
- knocked
- chocolate

Story starter

One morning, Harry heard that his teacher was ill and that a supply teacher was going to take the class. Harry was surprised when the classroom door opened and a man wearing a chef's hat ran in!

Beans for the Queen

The classroom door opened
and a chef ran in.

"Be quiet you lot!" he shouted.

"I am your teacher today.
You can call me Chef."

But the chef wasn't going to cook.
He was going to talk about
vegetables.

"Vegetables are boring!" said Harry.
"Be quiet!" shouted the chef.
"Vegetables are not boring. They are good for you!"

Then the chef's phone rang. It was the Queen. She wanted the chef to cook dinner for her – **now**! "If she doesn't like my cooking she will chop off my head," said the chef.

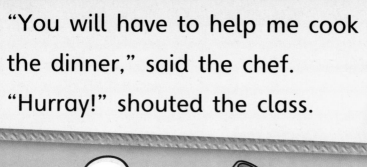

"You will have to help me cook the dinner," said the chef.
"Hurray!" shouted the class.

They all went with the chef to the palace.

"We have lots to do," said the chef. "You must peel and chop all the vegetables."

"Oh no!" said Harry. "That's boring!"

"Who said that?" shouted the chef
and he turned to Harry.
BANG! The chef hit his head on
a frying pan.
He was knocked out!

"Now who will cook dinner for the Queen?" said the class. "If she doesn't get her dinner, she will chop off our heads!"

Harry had an idea. "**We** will cook dinner for the Queen!" he said. "But we don't know how to cook," said the class.

Harry and the class made beans on toast and a chocolate milkshake for the Queen's dinner.

"What if the Queen doesn't like it?" said the class. "She will chop off our heads!"

What do you think will happen now?

The Queen came to see Harry and the class.

"That was the best dinner I have **ever** had," she said. "Hurray for Harry!"

Quiz

Text Detective

- Why was the chef afraid of cooking for the Queen?
- Do you think the Queen would really like Harry's dinner?

Word Detective

- **Phonic Focus:** Long vowel phonemes

  Page 24: Sound out the three phonemes in 'peel'. What long vowel phoneme can you hear?
- Page 25: Find three verbs ending in 'ed'.
- Page 27: Why is the word 'We' in bold print?

Super Speller

Read these words:

cook   wanted   who

Now try to spell them!

HA! HA! HA!

Q How do you stop someone from stealing fast food?

A Fit a burger alarm!